RAV DOVBER PINSON

A Bond for Eternity

understanding
THE BRIS MILAH

IYYUN PUBLISHING

Published by IYYUN Publishing
232 Bergen Street
Brooklyn, NY 11217

www.IYYUN.com

Iyyun Publishing books may be purchased for educational, business or sales promotional use. For information please contact: contact@IYYUN.com

cover and book design: Rochie Pinson

pb ISBN 978-0-9852011-9-7
Pinson, DovBer 1971-
A Bond for Eternity: Understanding the Bris Milah

1. Judaism 2. Spirituality 3. Holidays

RAV DOVBER PINSON

A Bond
for Eternity
understanding
THE BRIS MILAH

IYYUN PUBLISHING

B"H

THIS BOOK HAS BEEN WRITTEN AND PREPARED
AS A GIFT FOR A DEAR FRIEND AND DISCIPLE

Mr. Genaddiy
Tzvi Hirsh Bogolyubov
and his wife, Sonia

ON THE OCCASION OF THE BIRTH OF THEIR SON,
AND THE BRIS CEREMONY.

May they both know pure nachas from him
and all their lovely children in good health,
physical & spiritual abundance, and joy.

May he grow up to be a true 'Talmid Chacham' —
wise, open and loving, proudly and fearlessly walking
through the journey of life, while treading on the paved
path of his ancestors and bringing tremendous nachas to
his Parents, Grandparents, and Klal Yisrael

WITH BLESSINGS
Rav DovBer Pinson
NEW YORK, 2013

CONTENTS

⟨ ETERNAL BOND ⟩

THE ACT OF THE BRIS, 'CIRCUMCISION', IS ONE OF THE most fundamental acts of Judaism. It is an *Os*, a sign or signature, of entering into a covenant with the Creator.

A covenant is a pact. It could be considered like an agreement, usually a formal one, between two or more persons to do or not do something specified.

Yet, a covenant, as opposed to a more straightforward agreement or contract, is 'blindly' binding. In other words, it is non-conditional. Generally speaking, a person enters into a partnership, if it does not work out, it will either come to a natural and mutual end, or one party is forced out of the partnership by the other. A covenant, by definition, means an eternal relationship, one that can never be broken. The Bris, as a sign of entering into this covenant, is etched into the very fabric of our bodies, never to be forgotten as long as we live.

The Bris links us into an ancestral chain of history and tradition that bears witness to a sacred relationship that is beyond comprehension — both unconditional and eternally binding. This is the basic reason why the Bris is performed as we are infants — either literally, as in when we are babies, or figuratively, as in the case of a new convert, who is considered as if reborn from the waters of the Mikvah — demonstrating that this relationship is not founded on convention or rationale. It is deeply ingrained into the essence of who we are, acting upon the most sensitive organ that is the source of (future) life.

The Bris is an eternal bond, etched into our bodies, binding us to the Creator, enabling us to become part of the eternal nation of *Klal Yisrael*, the 'people of Israel'.

This physical link to a spiritual eternity is performed precisely upon the very body part that is overtly linked to our own, experience of eternity. Our lives are finite. We become embodied for a period of time, into a particular place, and than we pass on. Yet, one of the many forms of potential eternity is through the perpetuation of our genes through our children, and they in turn live on through their children. The sages of the Talmud call this the "Eternity of the species" *(Yerushalmi, Berachos,* 1:1*)*. The sign of our eternal bond with The Infinite One is marked on the very part of the body that brings us our —albeit finite — sliver of eternity. Our personal eternity is now linked with the eternity of our people, forever bound to the Eternal One.

The physical act of the Bris, removing the foreskin, is an act of revealing. In essence, the Bris does not forge this bond, but rather, it simply reveals what is already there.

WHY THE EIGHTH DAY?

"On the eighth day, the flesh of his foreskin must be circumcised" (Vaykira, 12:3).

NOT A DAY EARLIER, BUT ALSO NOT 'FROM THE EIGHTH day onward', but specifically on the eighth day itself.

Why the eighth day?

The Torah itself only instructs us to perform the Bris on the eighth day; it offers no explicit reason for doing this. The truth is, we do not need logical reasons for performing the Mitzvos, for they are rooted in the absolute simplicity of the Creator's Unity. Reasons suggest something extraneous to this simple Unity. On the other hand, we are fashioned by our Creator to seek meaning and to think and function in a binary mode, making sense of our experience through reason and intuition, contrast and correspondence, physical form and mystical symbol, history and prophecy. Therefore, while keeping Hashem's Simple Unity in mind, we will also explore some of the various 'reasons' for the eighth day.

Let us begin with the medical.

A MEDICAL REASON FOR THE EIGHTH DAY

While perhaps a mere external manifestation of a deeper spiritual reason, there is a fascinating medical phenomenon that occurs on the eighth day.

Within the human chemical makeup there is something that is called "vitamin K". We now know that Vitamin K is responsible for the production (by the liver) of the element known as prothrombin. Now, if there is a deficiency of Vitamin K there will be a deficiency in prothrombin and hemorrhaging may occur.

Conversely, it is Vitamin K, together with prothrombin, which causes blood coagulation, a very important ingredient in any surgical procedure.

Interestingly, between the second and fifth day of their life, a young infant is susceptible to bleeding, and only from the fifth day of life through the seventh day of life is there an adequate quantity of vitamin K, and thus prothrombin in the baby's system. Yet, amazingly, it is on the eighth day of life, and only on the eighth day, that the amount of prothrombin present is actually elevated above one hundred percent of normal. This is the only day in a male's life in which this will be the case; that he will have more than the normal amount of prothrombin in his system.

And so, the eighth day of life is in fact the perfect day for 'surgery', as prothrombin peaks and the blood coagulates and clots most smoothly.

So this is perhaps a physical, 'outer' manifestation of a deeper spiritual truth, the perfection of the eighth day for a Bris.

But what is the inner quality of the number eight, of the eighth day?

A HUMANISTIC REASON FOR THE EIGHTH DAY

The sages of the Talmud *(Nidah,* 31b*)* offer a social explanation for why the Bris is on the eighth day: so the parents of the child can share the joy and depth of this rite of passage together.

According to Torah law, for the first seven days following the birth of a son, the woman is considered *Tamei**, 'impure', and any relations between spouses is prohibited. On the eighth day they may resume normal relations and physical intimacy.

If, the Bris would be within the first seven days of birth, the celebration of the event would be limited for the parents, as they could not be intimate and share their joy together. And therefore, the Torah delays the Bris until the eighth day, so all related parties can fully participate in joy and love.

THE SYMBOLIC REASON FOR THE EIGHTH DAY

Every number or unit of numbers is symbolic of structures of process. One represents unity, two duality, three synthesis, and so forth.

Overall, the number seven represents the natural cycle of time, as revealed in the seven-day cycle of the week. Time is a fundamental property of our finite, dimensional universe. The cycle of time encapsulates the flow of nature. Whereas the number eight, the number beyond seven, represents that which is outside the natural order. Eight is the one *above* or *beyond* the seven of nature. The

---

*A note about *Tamei* and the concept of 'impure.' Tamei has to do with a connection with death. So while birth is the beginning of life for the child, for the mother who has birthed the baby, there is an experience of death, or absolute separation. Throughout the pregnancy, the mother is one with the fetus, a single living being. When the baby emerges as an individual being, the cord is cut and there is an intense separation, which may also be the source of post partum depression. This is a form of death for the mother, and therefore she enters a state of 'impurity'. A time of seven days of 'grieving', so to speak, mirroring Shiva, the seven days of mourning upon the passing of a loved one.

number eight literally symbolizes the "Supernatural", the potential and presence of the miraculous.

And yet, paradoxically, whereas eight represents transcendence, it also represents the human being's active participation in the perfection of nature, a co-creative completion, on our part, of creation.

Seven represents the Creator's completion of creation, as in, the "six days of creation". On the "seventh day", the Creator rested from the work of creation. Eight represents our collaborative "completion" of the Creator's creation.

Seven symbolizes the creation of the Creator. Eight signifies the creativity of that very creation.

Besides the Bris, the other prominent Eighth Day we find in the Torah is in relation to the *Mishkan*, the portable sanctuary of the Israelites in the desert. In the desert, after leaving Egypt, the Mishkan was dedicated on the Eighth day. The purpose of the Mishkan, explains the

Ramban, was to build and replicate on earth the inner structure of the cosmos, which was created in seven days— to replicate, via our creativity, the Creator's creation. Eight represents our participation, our creative process, mimicking the seven, the Creator's creation.

The meeting of these two dimensions is most pronounced in regard to the Bris, the circumcision on the eighth day. A male infant is born with a foreskin, uncircumcised. The way we are born is the way our Creator created us. Therefore, according to the Creator's creation, males are uncircumcised, and yet, we are given the Mitzvah (by the Creator), the special power and privilege, that on the eighth day we can complete, rectify, and repair the Creator's creation, as it were.

Once, Turnus Rufus, a Roman governor posted in Judea during the first half of the second century C.E., challenged the famous Talmudic scholar Rabbi Akiva to a debate (*Tanchumah*, Tazria. 5). "Whose deeds are greater?" he asked Rabbi Akiva, "the Creator or humankind?" Rabbi

Akiva answered, "Those of the human being." Turnus
Rufus continued his line of questions, "Why do you cir-
cumcise your male infants?" Rabbi Akiva responded that
he knew that this question was coming, and that was why
he answered the way he answered. But to prove the point
more fully, Rabbi Akiva brought several stalks of raw grain
along with a basket of beautiful baked cakes and said to
Turnus Rufus, "These stalks were made by the Creator,
while these cakes were produced by mortal man." Turnus
Rufus then reformulated his previous point: "If the Creator wants circumcision, why does the infant not leave the
womb circumcised?" Rabbi Akiva responded, "And why
does his umbilical cord come out still attached, with the
child hanging by his stomach until the mother cuts it?"
Rabbi Akiva then concluded, "The reason why people are
not born circumcised is because the Mitzvos were given
to refine us."

The *Mitzvos*, the commandments or practices, are given
to us in order to refine and elevate us, allowing us to participate in our own development and evolution.

We are thereby able to refine ourselves, taking part in our own creation.

Speaking of the creation of Adam, the primordial human being, the Torah says, *"And G-d said 'let us create man"* (*Bereishis*, 1:26).

The obvious question is, who is the 'us'? And why is it in the plural? Who is the Creator speaking to and about? Perhaps it is the royal we *(Rasag)*, or maybe G-d is speaking to the angels *(Rashi)*. But we may also say that the 'us' is literally 'us', meaning you and me. When we are being created the Creator speaks to us and empowers us, giving us the strength and responsibility, saying, "I want to create you, but I want you to be My partner in your very own creation."

There is the *created* perfection and the *creative* process inherent in our creation. By using our bodies and the physical tools we have been given, invested by the Creator with the power of, "let us create man," we are continually creating and recreating, shaping and evolving this Divine Creation.

This is the inner reason for the Bris on the eighth day, as eight is the *Yichud* or unity, between Transcendence and Immanence, between Perfection and Process, between Being and Becoming, between Creator—Creation—Creativity.

THE NAMING OF THE CHILD

ON THE EIGHTH DAY, AT THE BRIS, THE HIGHER LEVEL of our soul, our own personal and paradoxical piece of the Infinite, begins to enter our being. Our *Neshamah*, the Transcendent aspect of self, does not enter us fully at birth. Our soul's journey is engaged in a process of entry, as it were. At the Bris there is the first level of integration, the entry of our higher, deeper self into our bodies and into our consciousness. This is also the inner reason for the naming of the child at the Bris.

Our name is indicative of our inner essence and is often expressed in our personality and character (*Yuma*, 83b).

In truth, our name is a vessel that carries and maintains our soul, our personality, our purpose, and our identity. A name is the channel through which life flow reaches us from our Source. The name as a whole, as well as the specific letter and sound combination of the letters, is the conduit for which Divine energy flows to us and resonates with our deepest reality.

According to the *Arizal*, before parents name a child, (*Shar Hagilgulim*, Hakdamah 23) the parents experience a minor form of prophecy. They may have consciously chosen a name before the Bris, but the night before the day of the Bris, that name they chose will either resonate or not. Another name may appear. They may look at the child and say, "I see him as 'Baruch', or 'I feel like his name should be Gershon'". These are all aspects of prophecy, which is a form of higher and deeper intuition.

On the Eighth day, our Soul, our Transcendent Self, and thus, our ability to become more than we are, to grow, to dream, to evolve, enters fully into our body and being.

THE INNER REASON FOR THE EIGHTH DAY

DURING THE FIRST SEVEN DAYS OF LIFE THE *Kli* OR vessel, of who we are is being built, our bodies are still in the process of formation. It takes a 'seven day' cycle to create creation, and thus, to establish our own sense of embodied presence in this world.

To build a vessel takes seven days, as reflected in the seven' days of *Sheva Berachos* or seven blessings, after a wedding, and the seven-day cycle of healing after a death, the time of *Shiva*. Once the vessel is created, affirmed, and established, now, on the eighth day, an influx of *Ohr*,

Light, which represents our Soul and Transcendent Self, begins to penetrate our vessel, the body.

Seven is the natural cycle of sound (as in G-d created the world through speech); eight is the 'super-natural' cycle of light (as in the *Ohr Ein Sof,* the Light of Infinity). Seven is body, eight is soul. Seven is creation as it is, eight is creation as it should be.

To be in a *seven paradigm* is the acknowledgment of what is, to be in an *eight paradigm* is to dare to dream for more.

BODY & SOUL: THE DESIRE TO RECEIVE & THE DESIRE TO GIVE

A BRIS ON THE EIGHTH DAY COMPLETES THE PERSON beyond his creation at birth. A Bris consummates the person in a way that takes him beyond his nature (*Derech Chayim (Maharal)* Avos, 5:2).

We are all born with instincts for survival and self-preservation. As a by-product of self-preservation we are all born extremely selfish, with self-serving inclinations and instincts. This natural state, which is healthy and much needed, certainly in the first stages of existence as infants, we cry and throw tantrums when we are tired, hungry, or in pain. This behavior is a manifestation of our 'seven-day' reality, expressing the fundamental needs of our vessel, conveying our desire to receive what we need selfishly from life.

So while in infancy the natural desire to receive selfishly from life is much needed. Without crying when hungry, we may starve to death. Yet, the behavioral patterns of a selfish infant when left unchecked, become the behavioral issues of a toddler, later morphing into an entitled and overly demanding child, and finally a totally self-absorbed adult.

But this is not our whole story. We are born of *seven*, but have the potential of *eight*. We are both body and vessel (natural), but also soul and light (beyond nature).

Our bodies and instincts are selfish, they demand to be fed; yet, our inner core, our souls and inner light, are linked to the Source of all Blessing and Abundance, they are connected to and similar to that Source, and like that Source, they too desire to give to others, to offer ourselves, to live selflessly.

The nature of our vessels — our bodies, and the 'cycle of seven' manifested within Creation — is to receive for the self alone, selfishly feeding itself with more and more. The nature of the Light of our Souls, which is present within the potential of the 'eight', is to be like the Root of Light, the Creator, which is to give selflessly and mindfully, offering back to others even more than what we receive.

The dynamic is such: The body/the physical/the vessel is selfish, imbued with a relentless desire to receive and accumulate. The soul/inner light is selfless, invested with a desire to receive in order to give and to share.

Counter intuitively, the greatest gift we can give to give to others is our Self. Ultimately, we receive more lasting pleasure from giving than from receiving, because by giving we are accessing our deeper selves, and aligning our will with the Will of the Ultimate Giver, the Creator.

We are a composite of both vessel/body and light/soul. On the eighth day our soul begins to trickle down into our bodily awareness, slowly maturing and becoming more integrated over the course of our life journey. As we mature in age, and hopefully in understanding and wisdom, our soul reality becomes more and more assimilated into our whole being, eventually becoming more and more the guiding force of our life.

As the Bris takes place on the eighth day, two things are occurring:

1. The initiatory stage of the reception and integration of the light of our soul, our spiritual essence and connection to transcendence, which takes us beyond our natural selfish desires and instincts, and

2. The linking of our entire being with the nature-defying meta- historical narrative of *Klal Yisrael*, the People of Israel.

It is through the Bris that we enter into the Covenant of Avraham/Abraham and become a manifest member of Klal Yisrael. The Bris links us with Eternity and renders us supernatural. The People of Israel defy all linear logic, choosing and representing eternal life in the face of immanent death. By all estimations it is an historical anomaly, a miraculous demonstration within history that the People of Israel even exist, let alone prosper and flourish continuously and under all circumstances.

Whereas all the great nations and empires of old — the pyramid building Egyptians, the philosophically minded Greeks, the politically savvy Romans, the technologically advanced Babylonians — are all but extinct; the tiny stiff-necked nation of Israel, the Jewish people, representing less than one percent of the world's total population, has survived and striven to thrive. This is an historical miracle, defying the laws of natural history, whereby nations, like everything else in the natural world, go through the fundamental stages of development and demise — birth, maturity, and eventually death. The nation of Israel, after all these years, is still here, *Am Yisrael Chai.* Through the Bris, a baby boy becomes a revealed part of this great nature-defying nation.

WHY THE BRIS
IN THAT PART OF THE BODY?

THE RAMBAM WRITES THAT THE BRIS IS NOT INTENDED to complete the physical form of man, as all of nature is complete as created, but rather to fix or align man as a whole system.

By performing the Bris and revealing what was there all along, we are aligning our creative mental/spiritual potential with our created physical nature, thus evolving man to a higher level of integrated being — body and soul as one (*Morah Nevuchim*, 3:49). He writes that the physical act of circumcision, the removing of the foreskin, lessens the eventual pleasure of physical intimacy, and in effect, helps to curb and channel one's physical desires towards the experience and appreciation of the more subtle emotional and spiritual dimensions of loving relationship.

In the procedure of a Bris the foreskin is removed, so there is literally a lessening of the bodily organ, and as a result there is also a lessening of sensation. This is a double measure of lessening, both quantitative and qualitative.

Yet, precisely by this lessening, one is able to experience 'more'. There is a counterintuitive spiritual dynamic at play in this equation; where more leads to less, and where less is, in fact, more. The lessening of one dimension creates an increase on another.

TWO MODALITIES:

HISPASHTUS/EXPANSION LEADING TO TZIMTZUM/CONSTRICTION
VS.
TZIMTZUM/CONSTRICTION LEADING TO HISPASHTUS/EXPANSION

IT IS QUITE RARE, ALMOST NON-EXISTENT IN FACT, THAT a completely unrestrained or unrestricted approach to any experience is actually better. Most often some degree of restriction or discipline, a lessening of sorts, brings one to a more thorough enjoyment and appreciation of that experience, ultimately allowing one to access more of that particular experience.

To explain:

There are two modalities we can function in:

1. *Hispashtus* or Expansion, consists of unrestricted, untamed, non-responsible, free, and mindless behavior, which eventually leads to a inevitable total state of *Tzimtzum* or Constriction, limitation, wherein one experiences feelings of emptiness and even disgust.

2. *Tzimtzum* or Constriction, is the basis for a life style founded on the premise and principles of exercising discipline, limitations, and mindfulness, which, G-d willing, leads one to a healthy and productive state of true and liberating feelings of *Hispashtus*, expansion and openness.

The proper flow of creation is that Tzimtzum leads to Hispashtus. The restricting and withdrawal, as it were, of the Infinite Light brings about the expansion of the many facets of finite creation. Correspondingly, as we are created in the image of the Creator, we inherently function in much the same fashion. We inhale inwards in order to exhale outward, we bend down to jump up, we pull back to get the momentum to move forward.

These two paradigms, of Tzimtzum to Hispashtus or Hispashtus to Tzimtzum, filter into every aspect of our lives.

We can either approach life from a 'Tzimtzum to Hispashtus' perspective, or a 'Hispashtus to Tzimtzum' perspective.

Kedusha or sanctity, the appropriate inner flow of creation is maintained through the dictum that Tzimtzum leads to Hispashtus. Correspondingly, *Klipa* or concealment, identified as that which conceals the kernel of truth or inner nature of reality, works in reverse — Hispashtus leading to Tzimtzum. In simple terms, this means that most times, too much of a good thing actually leads to less enjoyment or appreciation of that good thing.

We all walk around with a gaping sense of existential emptiness, a bitter sense of lack, and we so desperately wish to fill this hole. We imagine that if only we get *this thing* or *that opportunity*, we can bridge this inner abyss. Maybe it is a new car, the newest iPad, the dream vacation, and yet, the more we try to fill our emptiness with things, the more we try to stuff ourselves with stuff, the bigger our hole becomes and the more empty we feel.

The more initial Hispashtus we exercise in our approach of an object or experience, the more restricted, limited, exhausted and disgusted we end up feeling. Indulging an appetite with no limitations, only to be left feeling repulsed by one's own hunger and lack of control. Eating or drinking until you throw up, or buying until you are broke.

Imagine, for example, you relish a particular food, say a piece of meat, and one day, someone comes over to you and tells you, "I will pay, and you can eat as much as you want!" And you go ahead and stuff yourself until you are bloated, nauseous, sick, and disgusted, afterwards promising yourself that you will never eat meat again in your life.

This is true of all human desires. Meat is but a metaphor for all forms of hunger and appetite. Try to fill your desires with no limitations, no boundaries, no sense of responsibility, and you will end up feeling more sick, more empty, and more unsatisfied than you were before you started.

The untamed or unhindered expression of Hispashtus eventually leads to an inevitable meltdown and state of total Tzimtzum, resulting in involuntary and reactive restrictions, contractions and feelings of smallness and emptiness.

The higher and deeper way of living, and in fact, the way macro- and microcosmic life and creation truly works, is to practice a degree of Tzimtzum in order to achieve an experience of Hispashtus. Simply put, by being or doing less, or at least approaching your being or doing in a more restricted and modest manner, you can often gain and experience more of what you desire. 'More' in this case mostly refers to quality, but even quantity.

A practical distinction between a 'Tzimtzum to Hispash-tus' approach, as opposed to a 'Hispashtus to Tzimtzum' approach, can be illustrated in the following example:

A person walks into a restaurant, sets a budget, or fixes the amount of dishes or calories he will eat, and than sits down to eat. Doing so will ensure that he will have a truly pleasurable meal. Having practiced Tzimtzum, resolving to eat only two courses or spend only 'x' amount of money, he enjoys a healthy and satisfying sense of accomplishment and Hispashtus. When he walks out of the restaurant he feels good and satiated.

Contrary to that series of events, a person walks into a restaurant with no set budget or ideal amount of food he would like to eat, orders everything on the menu, and then barely has the strength to get up from his seat. After that he may even literally or figuratively feel sick to his stomach. This is a person who lives a life of Hispashtus that constantly leads to more and more Tzimtzum.

The performance of the Bris leaves us with less, both literally in terms of flesh and figuratively in the form of sensation. It is an act of Tzimtzum, but one that brings us to a deeper sense of Hispashtus. Through this Tzimtzum we are able to access Hispashtus in a holier, more holistic, and wholesome way. Through the Bris our appetites related to the Bris, and in due time to our loving relationship with a spouse, will be channeled, focused, and truly pleasurable on multiple levels in a perfectly balanced state of Hispashtus.

The Inner Meaning of Orlah: Foreskin and its Removal

THE ESSENTIAL PROCEDURE OF THE BRIS IS TO REMOVE the *Orlah*, the foreskin, of the male organ. The word *Orlah* means something that is hidden (*Malbim*, Devarim, 30:11), or something that is closed off (*Tiferes Yisrael (Maharal)* Chap. 19. *Rashi*, Shemos, 6:12).

In the Torah, we find the term Orlah in reference to a handful of different concepts including the fruit of a tree within its first three years of life (*Vayikra* 19:23), the foreskin that is removed during circumcision (*Bereishis* 17:11), and in reference to removing the Orlah (metaphorical covering) of the heart (*Devarim* 10:16). In all three scenarios, the concept of Orlah suggests a covering over, a blocking or blockage of something within.

Within the body itself there are various forms of Orlah. The Medrash speaks of the four Orlah's of the body (*Medrash Rabbah*, Bereishis, 46:5).

There is the Orlah of the Ears (Yirmiyahu, 6:10), referring to a person who is closed off and shut down so that they cannot listen to what needs to be heard.

There is the Orlah of the Mouth (Shemos, 6:30), referring to a person who is unable to speak due to overwhelming trauma, for example, or some other experience in which he loses his ability to articulate what is bothering him.

There is the Orlah of the Heart (Yirmiyahu, 9:25), in which a person is intellectually and emotionally closed off from others.

And there is the Orlah of the Body, referring to the foreskin, which is removed during the Bris.

As mentioned, any fruits that grow during the first three years of a tree's life are considered Orlah, they are as if concealed and off limits to us. They are not to be eaten or enjoyed. Things need to be ripe before plucking. From a Kabbalistic frame of reference, for the first three years of a tree's life the fruits are not yet ready for human consumption. There are traces of impure spirits, unrefined and humanly inaccessible energies that are attached to the tree for the first three years, and thus, we are to refrain from using them for our personal benefit (*Zohar* 11. p. 244b. *Sharei Orah*, 5. *Pardes Rimonim*, 24. *Likutei Torah*. Kedoshim).

Adam, the primordial human being, before eating from the Tree of Knowledge of Good and Evil, before being inculcated into the realm of duality, did not posses an Orlah, he had no foreskin *(Pirkei D'Rabbi Eliezer)*. The sin of Adam, our sages tell us, is that he stretched his foreskin over his (natural) circumcision *(Sanhedrin, 38b)*. In addition, the Arizal teaches that Adam and Chava would have been permitted to enjoy the fruit, at a later time, on Shabbos.

This establishes a further connection between these two concepts of Orlah.

Before eating from the 'Tree of Knowledge good and evil', duality, Adam lived in the 'Tree of Life' reality — a life of simple unity, free of pain, suffering and death. He, and on a deeper level — we, before eating from the Tree of Duality, was a spiritual being with no unhealthy desires emanating from a place of emptiness, lack, or need, as everything in his world was unified and fulfilled. By eating, identifying, and internalizing the polarities of good and evil, he entered into a world of separation, including all that comes into stark focus and contrast due to this separation.

This is the inner reason why Adam did not have Orlah, foreskin, while living in the Tree of Life reality, as there was no separation, covering, or concealment. Once he identified with the Tree of Duality, once negativity and separation were internalized, and with them, the limitations of his five finite senses and the entrapment of his imagination, he stretched his foreskin and concealed his procreative organ. His body, which up until this point had been a transparent Body of Light, the garment of his soul, needed a covering or concealment to match the new psychological and spiritual layer of separation that had been initiated by the eating of the Fruit of Duality, and he thereby forced the foreskin over his circumcision, literally and figuratively.

Adam, in the Garden of Eden was told, *"From every tree of the Garden you may eat freely, but from the Tree of Knowledge of good and evil do not eat"* (*Bereishis*, 2:16-17).

These two statements seem to contradict each other. Either he could eat from every tree in the Garden, including the tree of knowledge, or he could not eat from every tree, in which case the statement, "from every tree of the Garden you may eat freely", is incorrect. What is meant by this?

The inner meaning of the above seemingly paradoxical statement is that: he can eat from every tree, but he should

A BOND FOR ETERNITY

not eat from one particular tree. He can eat everything, but he should not eat from just one specific thing.

For everything in the Garden contained both aspects, the Tree of Life and the Tree of Duality within it. Adam was told, "you can eat everything", this is the *tree of life*, "just do not eat something in specific", this approach represents the *tree of duality*. Because the moment you say, "I want this or that thing", the moment you choose to eat one particular thing over another, you are identifying with the Tree of Duality, for you are separating the one from the all, which is the Tree of Life and Unity.

But that is exactly what he (and sadly we) did (and do). He chose the 'one thing' over the 'everything', and he 'stretched his foreskin over his circumcision', creating for himself a paradigm of separation. He created a barrier, a cover, a garment, between himself and everything around him.

The stretching of the Orlah inwardly means that he placed a barrier between himself and all of life, he became

38

overwhelmingly self-aware and self-conscious. He was no longer at-one with himself or with the world around him.

This requires a fixing. This is the inner meaning of Teshuvah and atonement, i.e. returning to a state of at-one-ment.

Through the act of circumcision and removing of a *Klipa* — a separation, a covering, a concealment — particularly from this part of our body — that is intricately related to our relationship with our 'other half', our *Palga D'gufah* — we are performing a *Tikkun*, a rectification and repairing of this cosmic miscalculation.

Today, in our collective condition of exile and separation (both internal and external), we achieve our Tikkun through an actual circumcision. In the future, when both internal and external collective redemption will be realized, we will be born, as Adam was, literally or figuratively, with no Orlah, no foreskin, no separation or concealment.

With the Bris, we remove all negative concealments, *Dinim* or 'judgments', and Klipa.

The first person to perform the Bris was the patriarch Avraham/Abraham. In fact, today we call the Bris, the 'Covenant of Avraham'. The Bris is the covenant that founded the nation of Israel, beginning with Avraham, and ever since, with all those who belong to the nation. Through the act of the Bris, we become, in a revealed way, a part of the eternal people of Israel, the children of Avraham.

Before undergoing the circumcision, Avraham's name was Avram, which is comprised of two words, *Av*, father, and *Ram*, exalted. His name reflected his perception of life and his relationship with the Creator. To Avram, the Creator was a father who was *Ram* — removed, transcendent, exalted, and detached from the world. Fulfilling the Divine command to undergo a Bris, removing the veil from his own body and taking off the Orlah, literally and inwardly, he revealed Hashem's presence within his own flesh, within the immediate and tangible, within the physical. And so his name was transformed into Avraham, adding the letter *Hei* to Avram. Now with a Hei, the name stands for *Av Hamon (Goyim)*, the Father of Many Nations. Instead of an exalted and distant father, he is a father to many nations.

As a result of the Bris, Avraham begins to sense Hashem's presence within creation.

The word *Milah*, 'circumcision', can be divided into *Mal Yud-Hei*, where the word *Mal* means 'speech', as in speaking or revealing the *Yud-Hei*, the name of G-d, bringing down and expressing the Divine presence within the world as well as within the body. The Zohar calls the procreative organ the *S'yuma D'gufah*, the end of the body. The purpose of the Bris is to reveal the *Yud-Hei*, the presence of Hashem, in the 'end' of the body, to sense the Divine Presence within what could be considered the lowest part of the body.

Numerically the word Milah equals 85. The Hebrew word *Peh*, mouth, an opening, also equals 85. The idea of the Milah is to remove the foreskin in order to create and reveal an opening, thereby undoing the concealment, the Klipa, and revealing Hashem's presence within the immediacy of creation.

Practically, the idea of Hashem's presence in the body is manifest both as the physical mark of a Mitzvah imprinted within the body, as well as a signifier of what the Bris implies inwardly, a shift in consciousness towards the path that leads from Tzimtzum to Hispashtus, which is the holy, noble, integrated way of living.

The Kabbalah of Bris

THERE IS A MEDICAL ANOMALY, A PHYSICAL PHENOMENON that demands our attention. As we move into the sphere of the Kabbalah, the hidden, internal realms of reality, it often suites us well to focus our awareness on the external, the most blatant and obvious aspect of attention. Because often, to get a glimpse into the hidden and mysterious we need to first understand what is revealed and apparent. In other words, to truly appreciate a grand and panoramic vision, we first need to acknowledge what is right in front of our eyes.

The biological development of the human being is such that we all begin life as females. All bodies, medically speaking, are first female before some of them morph into males, while the rest remain in their original state. Initially, with all genders, the internal gonads are contained within the body, and only after eight weeks do the gonads begin to move downward, in the case of a male, to become the male organ of distinction.

Evidently, there is an aspect of the male within the female, and the same is true in reverse, every female contains a potential male. This physical phenomenon is an articulation and external manifestation and expression of an internal truth.

The Torah describes two narratives in the creation of Adam and *Chava* or Eve. In the First Chapter of *Bereishis*, Genesis, when it speaks about the creation of Adam and Chava, the Torah says, "Male and Female He Created them" (*Bereishis*, 1:27). Adam and Chava were created simultaneously, both male and female, in one body, with two faces, in a back to back position. Just to visualize, this is like dual-gendered Siamese twins connected at the back and facing in opposite directions.

Then in Chapter Two of *Bereishis*, again it repeats the narrative of the creation of Adam and Chava, but in this story Adam and Chava are created in separate events. Adam was created first, and then Chava.

On a deep level this means that in Chapter One of Bereishis, Adam and Chava were first created as one unit, existing within and attached to the other, in a position of *Achor B'Achor*, back to back.

Indeed, their relationship with each other was 'back to back', a relationship that is a constant, as in, always connected at the hip, as it were, but never a truly genuine encounter with the other, as the other is simply experienced as an extension of oneself. Parents often have this kind of relationship with their younger children. The child is completely dependent on the parent for food, shelter and love. The child is always present, and yet, it is not a genuine encounter, as it is always one sided. The parents control the relationship, and, metaphorically, their children are their extensions, their children are attached to their hip, wherever they move, so do their children.

Chapter Two in Bereishis explores a different and far deeper encounter, which is called *Panim El Panim*, a 'face to face' relationship. The second narrative of Adam and Chava's creation explores how Adam (who included Chava, as Chava included Adam) and Chava were severed from each other during the 'deep sleep' of Adam, which is known in the writings of the *AriZal* as the *Nesirah* or the severing, in order to become two separate human beings, and thus, to be able to have a genuine face to face encounter.

In the inner world of the *Sefiros* — the Divine emanations and attributes, the lenses through which Infinity permeates finitude, the filters through which the Infinite colorless, formless, and unified light is reflected into our tangible world of multiplicity — there are various *Partzufim*. A *Partzuf* is a persona, or complete unit of Sefiros. There is the 'masculine' Partzuf of *Zah* — the six emotional Sefiros — and there is the Partzuf of *Nukvah* — the 'feminine'. Prior to the *Nesirah*, the severing, the Partzuf of Zah was complete with both masculine and feminine aspects.

In the primordial state, as illustrated in Chapter One of Bereishis, Adam and Chava are one. Originally, in our primordial state, there is the *Hiskalelus* or inter-inclusion, of male and female as one. Then, as manifest within our physical reality, male and female separate, and yet, deep within, each one contains its opposite.

To connect to and have a relationship with an opposite, whether in the form of a person or an idea (an object or a subject), there needs to be an implied corollary, a commonality between you and the other person or idea.

One needs to find and reveal that opposite within oneself so that they can identify with and then have a connection to that opposite.

In interpersonal relationships, in order for there to be a flourishing relationship between two, opposite, 'face to face' people in a sacred and healthy marriage, the masculine needs to reveal the feminine quality deep within himself in order to be able to acknowledge and honor the inherent inter-inclusion of available energies, and thereby establish that corollary and connection with the feminine other. Of course, this is equally true for the feminine principle as well.

Masculine and feminine are, in addition to physical expressions, also forms of mental and psychological principles. A masculine expression is linear, goal oriented, always wanting to do something about the problem. This is symbolic of a line, a logical progression from point A to point B. A feminine expression is cyclical, process oriented, receptive, always needing to speak about the issue. This is symbolic of a circle and a process.

In our primordial state, Adam and Chava are one. Yet, following the Nesirah, there is a separation and resulting duality of gender. Although, the ultimate purpose of this separation is to create a dynamic tension, which in turn brings about a greater level of unity — a unity of face-to-face relations and shared power within love.

This illuminates a deeper significance of the Bris. The Bris is performed on the male body part that overtly distinguishes the genders. *Zah*, the masculine, is manifest within the *Yesod*, foundation, of the male body, which is a line. Through the Bris, the foreskin is removed from the 'end of the line', so to speak, in order to reveal the *Atarah* or 'crown' of *Yesod*, a rounded image, thus completing the masculine by revealing the feminine aspect within.

The Bris is another, deeper form of *Nesirah*, or severing and cutting off, which is in some ways similar to the cutting of the umbilical cord, an act that separates the mother (feminine principle) from the male baby (masculine principle). But with the Bris, the severing is meant to support the intended revealing of the feminine within the masculine. This revealing, it is taught, will serve to assist the future young man as he seeks to identify his *Bashert*, his feminine 'other half'.

The Nesirah on one level ultimately leads to a greater and deeper *Yichud*, unification, on another level. In the words of the Torah regarding Adam, "Then Adam said (after the Nesirah, the 'separation' of Adam from Chava, resulting in the emergence of two separate people), 'This is now bone of my bones and flesh of my flesh; she shall be called 'woman', for she was taken out of man'. And because she was taken out of man, from within, therefore, "A man will leave his father and mother and be united to his wife, and they will become one flesh [again, but on a higher level]" (*Bereishis*, 2:23-24).

Beyond the symbolism of revealing the feminine within the masculine, which by itself has a profound effect on one's consciousness if deeply contemplated, the actual physical Bris, in a tangible way, provides a feminine sensitivity to the masculine body. The actual Bris, the removal of the Orlah, foreskin, diminishes the physical sensation, as the Rambam writes. This in essence reigns in and tempers the aggressive masculine testosterone-loaded nature. Because of this lessening of sensation, the male is potentially able to reveal a more sensitive side, initiating a domestication of sorts. There is a sensitizing of the masculine to the feminine quality, and eventually — because he has physically, psychologically, and certainly spiritually, reigned in his instinctual aggression — when the baby becomes older he will be able to cultivate and foster a more harmonious and tender loving relationship with his future spouse.

White/Chesed - Red/Gevurah

"There are three partners in the creation of the human being — The Creator, a father and a mother. The father supplies the white substance out of which is formed... the mother supplies the...red substance out of which is formed..." (*Gemara*, Nidah, 31a).

Essentially, we learn from this passage in the Gemara that the father is connected with 'white', whereas the mother is associated with 'red'. But what does this mean?

The discriminating body parts that distinguish a male from a female are also connected to these two colors — the seminal fluid is the white substance emanating from the male, whereas blood is the red substance, which emerges from the female, both in a monthly cycle as well as during birth.

Overall, the *Sefiros* are associated with ten variant colors, with each *Sefira* being represented by another color — although clearly, there are no actual definitive colors to multi-dimensional spiritual realities. But in general, the color white is related to *Chesed*, and red is connected with *Gevurah*.

Chesed is normally translated as kindness, but more appropriately in this context, Chesed means the aspect of giving. *Gevurah*, which is generally translated as strength, severity, or restriction, in this context can be more aptly understood as the aspect of receiving.

The creation of a child necessitates three partners, the Creator bestowing the child with a soul (a "part of the One Above"), and a mother and father providing the egg and the seminal fluid. In Kabbalistic terms this means that the father contributes the white (Chesed/Giving), and the mother absorbs and nourishes the 'white' into and through the flow of the red (Gevurah/Receiving). These two opposing qualities fit and complement each other, allowing for the creation of a third, the child.

> White is Chesed, father, male, line, giving.
> Red is Gevurah, mother, female, circle, receiving.
> Working together in unison, a child is created.

Though it may appear as an inevitable by-product, the blood of the child going through the Bris is essential to his spiritual transformation. The Medrash speaks of the blood of the Bris as a type of offering, similar to an offering in the Temple (*Pirkei d'Rabbi Eliezer,* Ch. 29). The stark image of the red blood is integral to the process of the spiritual evolution being experienced by the one going through the Bris.

Through the Bris, as previously explained, an *Atarah* or crown of the Yesod, the 'masculine body part', is revealed. Manifestly, this means that a circle is created within a line. In the process of removing the *Orlah,* foreskin, which is a

Klipa, concealment, there is a release of Gevurah in the form of red blood. The procedure forces blood to flow from the Yesod, thus revealing a *Nukvah* or feminine quality, in *Duchrah*, the masculine. The Bris expunges, symbolically and tangibly, any negative aspect of Red/Gevurah from the body part that is associated with White/Chesed.

This act of both releasing and revealing Gevurah, as blood, in a place where Chesed is dominant, is also for the intention of removing all negative Gevurah that may reside. So the purpose of the Bris is two-fold: to release any trace of negative Gevurah from within Yesod, as well as to reveal and call forth the potential for positive Gevurah and its proper balance with the resident Chesed within Yesod. This provides an harmonic convergence of elements and energies necessary for a healthy psychological, physical, and spiritual constitution.

Chesed and Gevurah are only positive when balanced, as they exist in the world of *Tikkun* or rectified reality. Unbalanced Gevurah and unbalanced Chesed are negative. Giving with no limitation or consideration for the recipient is negative Chesed. Paradoxically, in the Torah, an aggressive act of physical intimacy, Heaven forbid, without the consent of the recipient, is called a "Chesed". This runs counter to our general understanding of Chesed, which is the loving quality of pure giving. But that definition is only based on a rectified Chesed. An unrectified Chesed, from the world of *Tohu* or Chaos, as opposed to Tikkun, results in a form of giving with no acknowledgement or respect for the needs or desires of the receiver. And hence, the manifestation of such a shameful and abominable act, expressing a perverse form of Chesed with no Gevurah, is the result.

Unbalanced Gevurah without any Chesed on the other hand, can lead to the state of complete restriction, wherein there is no possibility of giving, where one is completely closed off and shut down.

The Bris releases all the latent negative Gevurahs, all unbalanced restrictions, *Dinim*, or judgments, and concealments, allowing the child to develop a balanced Chesed in sync with a healthy Gevurah.

Releasing the negative Gevurah (represented as blood) through the Bris, in effect, also enhances and enforces a more positive relationship to Gevurah — a sense of constructive and positive constriction, and an awareness of and sensitivity to when to say no, or to not do something that is not wanted.

The Bris lessens, holds back, and diminishes (which is an act of Gevurah) the free flow of unbalanced and negative Chesed by reducing some of the physical sensation, and thus allowing for a more balanced and less aggressive 'feminine' modality of relationship with one's (eventual) spouse.

In this context, Gevurah can also be understood as *Tzimtzum*, a withdrawal, holding back, or restriction. But, as explained earlier, only through a balanced and focused Tzimtzum can there be a healthy and productive expression of Chesed, giving, and *Hispashtus*, expansion. Remember, the initial Tzimtzum leads to a finer form of eventual Hispashtus.

It is the male who ultimately needs to release such excess negative Gevurah, and thus, in the process, to reveal the concealed potential for positive Gevurah.

A note of importance: Overall, in generalized terms, the male's connection to and balancing of Chesed — giving, extroverting, moving forward —with the more feminine aspect of Gevurah — holding back, withdrawing, receiving — is not as natural as that of the female, and is in need of the Bris to rectify this imbalance.

The female, on the other hand, embodies both Gevurah and the counter-balance quality of Chesed naturally. In the words of the sages of the Talmud, "Women are naturally circumcised" (*Avodah Zarah*, 27a). Women, though rooted in Gevurah (the ability to receive), embody the masculine element of Chesed (the ability to give) effortlessly. In effect, they are already 'circumcised', or, one can say that they already embody the essence of the sought after spiritual effect of the Bris. So naturally do women embody a balanced sense of Chesed in fact, that, as it shines through the prism of Gevurah, it may actually appear to be their dominant attribute.

Men, on the other hand, are rooted in Chesed and yet are in dire need of being checked, controlled, steered, and guided in the course of their emotional development. Because the quality of Gevurah does not come to them naturally (i.e. they are not born with a Bris), they often tend to overcompensate and overwhelm their inherent inclination to express the positive qualities of Chesed, and instead present a hard and impenetrable shell of Gevurah to the outside world. This can be referred to as 'character armor', the psychological and social defense mechanisms people erect to protect themselves from an apparently threatening world, and even sometimes, unwittingly, from their deepest selves. Because this is not a natural or authentic expression of Gevurah, and men do in fact need strong Gevurah to tamper their inherent Chesed, many men end up appearing as more connected to Gevurah than women.

Often women, who are rooted and possess an innate connection to Gevurah, yet are balanced with a natural inclination for Chesed, appear more effortlessly giving, more thoughtful, gentler and kinder. While men who are rooted in Chesed by nature, often appear more as a caricature of an unbalanced sense of Gevurah, almost comically tougher and harder on the outside.

But it is through the Bris that there is a great Tikkun and 'sweetening' for the male. All negative Gevurah, if the Bris is done correctly, is expunged, and the male will now have the opportunity to reveal a properly balanced Chesed in harmony with a healthy Gevurah.

The Ceremony, The Sandek & Seat of Elijah the Prophet

THE ACTUAL CEREMONY OF THE BRIS HAS VERY POWERFUL spiritual significance, not only for the child or parents, but for all those in attendance. The Zohar teaches that at a Bris, negativity is removed and a shield of protection is fashioned for the baby and for all those in attendance.

So much so, that someone who has been invited to partake in someone else's Bris is not supposed to decline the invitation. For this reason, people do not directly invite others to a Bris, but rather, just let the word out, so as not to impose.

A Bris is a time of physical removal, and thus, potentially, a time for spiritual removal of all extraneous negative energy. Removal of all that is holding us back from living our deepest truth, whether it be fear, anger, regret, or anything else.

There are various different customs at the Bris, ranging from the custom of the *Kvatters*, a male and female messenger of the parents — usually spouses — who bring the baby into the room of the circumcision (this is a *segulah* or spiritual omen, for familial fertility), to the Sephardic custom of bringing the baby into the room with music. There is the custom of holding the baby on a beautifully decorated pillow, as well as the custom to make a blessing and smell fragrant spices at the Bris.

One of the oldest and most universal customs is to place a seat for *Eliyahu HaNavi*, Elijah the Prophet. In fact, a number of years back, many synagogues had a permanent ornamental chair dedicated for the Bris. The *Sandek**, the one who holds the child during the actual Bris, either sits on the seat of Eliyahu or on a seat nearby, and the seat of

Eliyahu remains empty. At a Bris, it is taught that whomever stands near the Seat of Eliyahu is forgiven and absolved from all of their past sins and negativity.

After the actual procedure of the Bris everyone present sits down to a Seudah, a 'festive meal'. Joy is an essential element of the Bris. The Bris is a Mitzvah that was accepted with joy and is still performed with joy (*Shabbos*, 130a); joy is essentially synonymous with the Bris (*Megilah*, 16b). This joyful meal, following the Bris is a very important aspect of the ceremony, not to be taken lightly. The *Arizal* teaches that a Bris with the meal that follows contains purifying spiritual energy equal to the merit and energy earned from forty days of fasting. But instead of fasting, there is feasting.

---

*A word about the Sandek: Overall, the Sandek should be a pious and spiritual person. Being a Sandek is likened to the role of the *Kohen Gadol* or High Priest, offering the holiest incense in the Temple. Positive qualities of the Sandek are transmitted to the baby during the Bris. The Sandek is essentially the *Kli* or the vessel, that supports and holds all of the energy that becomes revealed and available through the Bris. The purer, clearer, more focused, and integrated the Sandek is, the better the vessel.

OTHER BOOKS BY RAV DOVBER PINSON

Rav Pinson's books are available in all fine book stores and on the web.

REINCARNATION AND JUDAISM
The Journey of the Soul

INNER RHYTHMS
The Kabbalah of Music

MEDITATION AND JUDAISM
Exploring the Jewish Meditative Paths

TOWARD THE INFINITE
The Way of Kabbalistic Meditation

JEWISH WISDOM OF THE AFTERLIFE
The Myths, the Mysteries & Meanings

UPSHERIN
Exploring the Meaning of a Boy's First Haircut

THIRTY – TWO GATES OF WISDOM
Awakening through Kabbalah

THE PURIM READER
The Holiday of Purim Explored

EIGHT LIGHTS
8 Meditations for Chanukah

THE IYYUN HAGADAH
An Introduction to the Haggadah

THE MYSTERY OF KADDISH
Understanding the Mourner's Kaddish

PASSPORT TO KABBALAH
A Journey of Inner Transformation

RECLAIMING THE SELF
The Way of Teshuvah

THE FOUR SPECIES
The Symbolism of the Lulav & Esrog

THE GARDEN OF PARADOX:
The Essence of Non Dual Kabbalah

WRAPPED IN MAJESTY
Tefillin- Exploring the Mystery

ABOUT THE AUTHOR

Rav DovBer Pinson is a world-renowned Torah scholar, author, and beloved spiritual teacher. He is widely recognized as one of the world's foremost authorities on authentic Kabbalah and Jewish wisdom.

Through his books, lectures and seminars he has touched and inspired the lives of thousands throughout the globe.

He is the Rosh Yeshivah of the IYYUN Yeshiva and Dean of the IYYUN Center in New York.

www.ingramcontent.com/pod-product-compliance
Lightning Source LLC
Chambersburg PA
CBHW030500100426
42813CB00002B/287